Scale Chord Relationships

A Guide to Knowing What Notes to Play—and Why!

by Michael Mueller and Jeff Schroedl

To access audio visit:
www.halleonard.com/mylibrary

Enter Code
4549-0011-8983-0354

ISBN 978-0-634-01994-4

HAL•LEONARD®
CORPORATION

7777 W. BLUEMOUND RD. P.O. BOX 13819 MILWAUKEE, WI 53213

Visit Hal Leonard Online at
www.halleonard.com

Introduction

Think about all the obstacles that we as practicing guitarists face in our quest to make great music: technique, sightreading, learning the fretboard, ear training. But perhaps the most misunderstood skill of all is determining which notes we can play over which chords. For instance, what would you do if you were asked to take a solo over a chord progression that went from E to C#m to A to B? If you're like many beginner and intermediate guitarists, you may be hard-pressed finding one scale that would work, nevermind being able to come up with multiple options.

The truth is, for those who wish to improvise beyond the "hunt and peck" method, knowing the relationships between scales and chords is essential. After all, you can learn ten ways to play a B Mixolydian scale, but if you don't know when and where to play it, what's the use? Fortunately, the principles involved in scale-chord relationships apply to all forms of music. From rock and metal to jazz and blues, once you learn the nuts and bolts, you'll be all set to go.

Scale Chord Relationships provides the theoretical and harmonic tools necessary for you to fearlessly face improvisation opportunities as they arise. You'll be able to instantly (or darn close to it) recognize keys, analyze and interpret chord progressions, and quickly determine your best course of action to solo over any set of chord changes. So grab your guitar, tune up, and prepare to conquer the realm of scale-chord relationships.

Contents

1 Basic Harmony

Although most of us already know how to play chords on the guitar, the intricacies of how scales and chords interrelate are often ignored, largely due to frustration on the learner's part. Admittedly, it takes a good amount of work to understand these relationships at a musically functional level. This study of the structure, progression, and relationships of chords is termed *harmony*.

Major Scales

Before we start diving into chord construction and progressions, it is vital that we understand scale construction—particularly the major scale. The *major scale* consists of seven notes arranged in fixed intervals of whole and half steps:

$$1 - 2 - 3 - 4 - 5 - 6 - 7 - \text{Octave}$$
$$\text{W} \quad \text{W} \quad \text{H} \quad \text{W} \quad \text{W} \quad \text{W} \quad \text{H}$$

This relationship always exists in every major scale. For example, if we were to begin on the note C, the second degree would be one whole step higher, or D. The distance between the second and third tones is also a whole step, so the third degree is E. Next, you only need to progress one half step to reach the fourth degree, F. The fifth degree is one whole step higher than F, which is G. Go up another whole step to A for the sixth degree. The seventh degree is B, which is one whole step higher than A. Finally, to reach the octave (C), you need go up one half step. Let's add the notes of the C major scale to the diagram from above:

$$1 - 2 - 3 - 4 - 5 - 6 - 7 - \text{Octave}$$
$$\text{W} \quad \text{W} \quad \text{H} \quad \text{W} \quad \text{W} \quad \text{W} \quad \text{H}$$
$$\text{C} - \text{D} - \text{E} - \text{F} - \text{G} - \text{A} - \text{B} - \text{C}$$

Keys and Key Signatures

In western music, there are 12 tones between a root note and its octave, and you can form a major scale beginning on any one of these 12 tones. Thus, there are 12 major keys in western music, each with its own distinct key signature. A key refers to a system of notes, or chords for the purposes of this book, that are related to a common tonic note or chord. The *key signature* is a set of sharps or flats found immediately to the right of the clef sign in standard notation. The key signature not only tells you which notes are to be flatted or sharped throughout the musical piece, but also tells us what key the song is in. As you'll see later in this book, that information is invaluable when determining which scales to play for your improvisations within a song.

Fig. 1

Conveniently, the sharps and flats always appear in a certain order in the key signature, thus making memorization and analysis much easier. The order of sharps is: F♯–C♯–G♯–D♯–A♯–E♯–B♯.

To determine the key from the key signature, locate the final sharp and move up one half step. That note is the tonic. For example, if there are four sharps in the key signature (F♯–C♯–G♯–D♯), you should identify D♯ as the last sharp, move up one half step to E, and *voila*, you've analyzed the key signature as the key of E major.

Fig. 2

The order of flats is simply the the order of sharps in reverse: B♭–E♭–A♭–D♭–G♭–C♭–F♭

To determine the key from a key signature containing flats, simply locate the next-to-last flat, and its name is the tonic. For example, if there are three flats in the key signature (B♭–E♭–A♭), E♭ is the next-to-last flat and is thus the tonic, so you're in the key of E♭ major. There is an exception to this rule: If there is only one flat in the key signature (B♭), there isn't a "next-to-last" flat. You'll just need to memorize that one flat represents the key of F major.

Refer to the table below for a summary of the 12 major keys. Notice that there are actually 15 scales spelled out. The keys of B/C♭, F♯/G♭, and C♯/D♭ are what we call *enharmonic* equivalents; even though the pitches are spelled out differently, they share the exact same sound. So together, these six scales are considered as only three different scales.

Fig. 3

Major Key	1(tonic)	2(9)	3	4(11)	5	6(13)	7	8
C major	C	D	E	F	G	A	B	C
G major	G	A	B	C	D	E	F♯	G
D major	D	E	F♯	G	A	B	C♯	D
A major	A	B	C♯	D	E	F♯	G♯	A
E major	E	F♯	G♯	A	B	C♯	D♯	E
B major	B	C♯	D♯	E	F♯	G♯	A♯	B
C♭ major	C♭	D♭	E♭	F♭	G♭	A♭	B♭	C♭
F♯ major	F♯	G♯	A♯	B	C♯	D♯	E♯	F♯
G♭ major	G♭	A♭	B♭	C♭	D♭	E♭	F	G♭
C♯ major	C♯	D♯	E♯	F♯	G♯	A♯	B♯	C♯
D♭ major	D♭	E♭	F	G♭	A♭	B♭	C	D♭
A♭ major	A♭	B♭	C	D♭	E♭	F	G	A♭
E♭ major	E♭	F	G	A♭	B♭	C	D	E♭
B♭ major	B♭	C	D	E♭	F	G	A	B♭
F major	F	G	A	B♭	C	D	E	F

Triads

The most fundamental unit of harmony is a three-note chord, or *triad*. In all, there are four types of triads: major, minor, augmented, and diminished. The first two types, major and minor, are by far the most important, accounting for probably 95% of most music. A *major* triad is constructed from the first, third, and fifth notes (formula: 1–3–5) of the major scale. *Minor* triads require a small but critical change: flatting the third degree of the scale, which results in a formula of 1–♭3–5. The *augmented* triad is constructed from the first, third, and *sharp* fifth (formula: 1–3–♯5), and the *diminished* triad is the same as the minor triad but the fifth is flatted (formula: 1–♭3–♭5).

Figs. 4A and 4B contain all four of these triads constructed from the C major scale and E♭ major scale, respectively.

Fig. 4A

C major   C minor   C augmented   C diminished

Fig. 4B

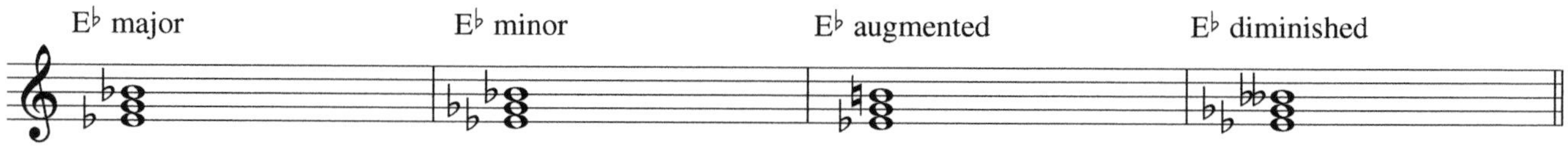

E♭ major   E♭ minor   E♭ augmented   E♭ diminished

Notice that the diminished triad in the E♭ example contains a B♭♭. This presents an ideal opportunity to discuss enharmonic equivalents and appropriate labeling in harmony. In harmonic theory, it is proper to alter the note using its original name as found in the root scale. So, in the example above, though it might be tempting to think of the 5th of the E♭ diminished chord as "A," it is harmonically correct to refer to it as "B♭♭." In Figs. 5A and 5B, try building each of the four triad types in G major and E major. The scales are provided above the staff.

Fig. 5A G major scale: G–A–B–C–D–E–F♯

Fig. 5B E major scale: E–F♯–G♯–A–B–C♯–D♯

Now that you've mastered the four triad types, let's further examine the relationship between the major scale and chords by harmonizing the major scale. This process determines the seven diatonic triads that naturally appear within a given key. We build the triads by stacking notes in thirds (*tertian harmony*). This can be accomplished by simply skipping one scale degree between chord tones (e.g., 1–3–5 skips 2 and 4). Let's start by harmonizing the C major scale.

Fig. 6

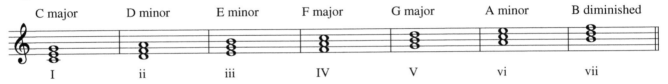

Notice the Roman numerals used to label a triad's location within the key. This is a generic method for labeling diatonic chords in any key. Also, notice that some are upper case, some are lower case, and one has a degree symbol (°) next to it. These treatments signify the chord quality: upper case reflects a major chord, lower case a minor chord, and lower case with the ° symbol a diminished chord. In diatonic major scale harmony, these qualities will always be the same. The I, IV, and V chords will always be major, the ii, iii, and vi chords will always be minor, and vii° will always be a diminished chord.

In the next chapter, you'll learn a method to help you identify a song's key using this Roman numeral system in conjunction with as little as two given chords. This will enable you to instantly identify the song's key as well as the diatonic chords in that key.

2 The Puzzle System

We presented the major scale and its harmonization in the previous chapter for a good reason. Armed with that info, you can save yourself a lot of extraneous work in your improvisation because you won't have to change scales each time you encounter a new chord! Using the information from chapter 1, it's possible to examine a chord progression and, working backwards, figure out the key in which those chords belong. As a result, you'll be able to improvise over a chord progression using only the major scale from that particular key. The method used to determine this "one scale fits all" concept is similar to working a puzzle.

Fig. 7

Positions	1	2	3	4	5	6	7
Chord Quality	major	minor	minor	major	major	minor	diminished

As you can see, the seven pieces correspond with the positions and chord qualities we discussed in chapter 1. Here's how the system works. First identify the chords in the music over which you're going to improvise. We'll use the chord progression in Fig. 8 as a working example.

1 Fig. 8

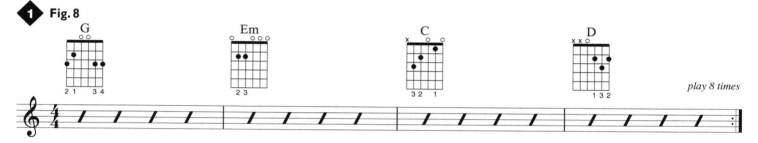

play 8 times

Now, let's place them in the puzzle system (Fig. 9). Remember: The chords must correspond to seven pieces of the puzzle both alphabetically and in terms of quality. That is, major chords can only fit into positions 1, 4, and 5; minor chords can only fit into positions 2, 3, and 6; and diminished chords can only be placed in position 7. In our above example, we can determine that since C and D follow alphabetically and are both major in quality, they can only be placed in positions 4 and 5. So enter C and D into those positions. Since Em is a minor chord, and it follows D alphabetically, we can enter it into position 6. Finally, G is a major chord, and the only remaining major chord spot is position 1. By working backward from C (i.e., C–B–A–G), you'll find that G does indeed belong in position 1, so place it there now.

Fig. 9

Position	1	2	3	4	5	6	7
Chord							

Often, a chord progression (or even an entire song) will only contain three or four chords, so we may not be able to account for all of the puzzle spots. For the sake of learning, however, it's still a good idea to fill in the remaining spots, so let's do that now with our example. First, we'll write out the G major scale: G–A–B–C–D–E–F♯. Position 2 is a minor quality, and A is the second degree of the scale, so fill in that blank with an Am chord. Position 3 is also minor, and B is the third degree, so Bm goes there. Finally, position 7 is diminished, and F♯ is the seventh scale degree, so place an F♯° chord symbol there. You now have a completed puzzle of the triads diatonic to the key of G.

So what does all this mean? Well, you now know that you can play a G major scale over the entire chord progression G–Em–C–D because those four chords use only notes from the G major scale. Try jamming along with the progression, using notes from the G major scale for your solo. For more practice, try tackling the chord progressions in Figs. 10–12. Use the puzzle system for each progression to determine the key and the scale you would use to solo in that key. The answers are provided in the appendix, but don't cheat! Once you've analyzed all three progressions, practice your solo skills by jamming along with the audio, using the appropriate scale for each progression.

2 Fig. 10

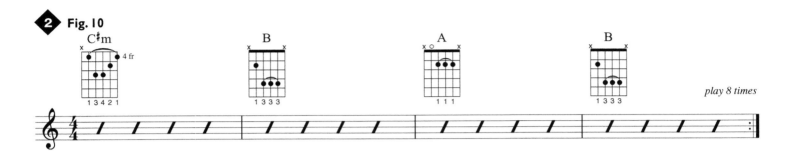

Position	1	2	3	4	5	6	7
Chord							

Key = ____

3 Fig. 11

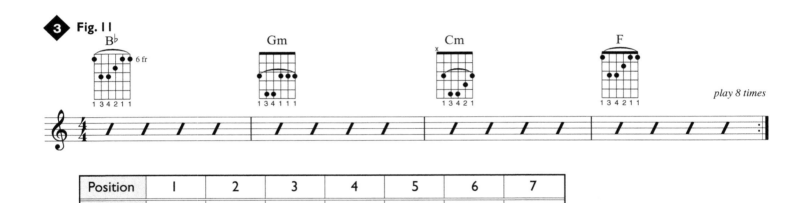

Position	1	2	3	4	5	6	7
Chord							

Key = ____

4 Fig. 12

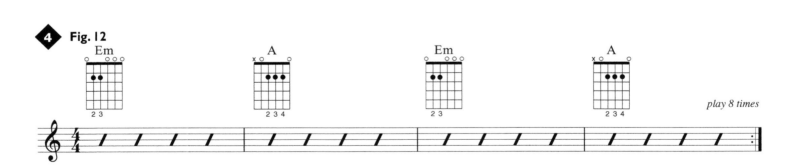

Position	1	2	3	4	5	6	7
Chord							

Key = ____

3 Seventh Chord Harmony

Chord Qualities

As you may already know, many songs contain chords other than simple triads. Jazz, in particular, often uses seventh chords to provide more harmonic "color" to a progression. Remember there are four types of triads: major, minor, augmented, and diminished. In seventh chord construction, there are seven chord types you should be familiar with. Check out the table in Fig. 13 for a summary of seventh chord types and their construction.

Fig. 13

Harmonic analysis of seventh chords uses the same basic process as triads, but there is an alter-

Types	Formula	Spelling (C as root)	Symbols
major seventh	1–3–5–7	C–E–G–B	Cmaj7, CM7, C △7
dominant seventh	1–3–5–♭7	C–E–G–B♭	C7, Cdom7
minor seventh	1–♭3–5–♭7	C–E♭–G–B♭	Cm7, Cmin7, C -7
minor seven flat five (half-diminished seventh)	1–♭3–♭5–♭7	C–E♭–G♭–B♭	Cm7♭5, Cø7
diminished seventh	1–♭3–♭5–♭♭7	C–E♭–G♭–B♭♭(A)	C7, Cdim7
augmented seventh	1–3–♯5–♭7	C–E–G♯–B♭	C+7, C7♯5, Caug7
minor/major seventh	1–♭3–5–7	C–E♭–G–B	Cm(maj7), C -(maj7)

ation to the chord qualities within the puzzle system. Let's start by harmonizing an F major scale using seventh chords.

Fig. 14

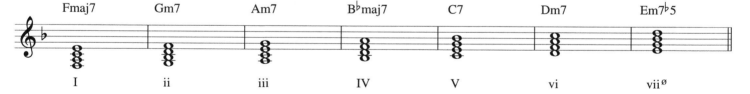

Notice that the chord qualities are the same as the harmonized triads with the exception of positions 5 and 7, which were major and diminished in quality, respectively, in triadic harmony. By introducing the seventh scale degree, we encounter two new chord qualities: the dominant chord (1–3–5–♭7) in position 5 and the half-diminished chord (1–♭3–♭5–♭7), also commonly called a "minor seven flat five" chord in position 7. Additionally, the major triads in positions 1 and 4 become major seventh chords, and the minor triads in positions 2,3, and 6 become minor seventh chords.

Organizing Progressions with Seventh Chords

The dominant seventh chord has a critical role in harmonic analysis. Whenever it appears in a diatonic progression, you know right away that it belongs in position 5. This handy rule takes a lot of the initial guesswork away in filling the puzzle spots. Let's work our way through a real example to demonstrate how it works.

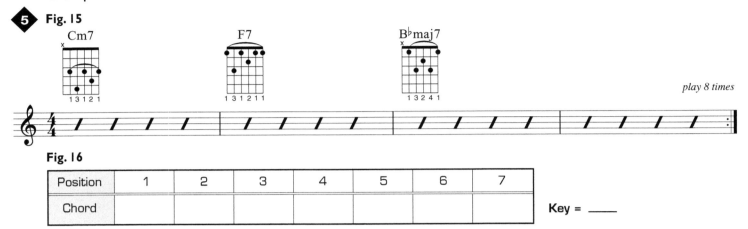

Fig. 15

play 8 times

Fig. 16

Position	1	2	3	4	5	6	7
Chord							

Key = _____

Since this chord progression contains a dominant seventh chord (F7), we can place that in position 5 of the puzzle right off the bat (Fig. 16). That leaves the B♭maj7 and Cm7 chords. We know that positions 1 and 4 are the only major qualities, so B♭maj7 belongs in one of those. Remember, the chords have to follow alphabetically, too, so it's impossible for B♭maj7 to fit in position 4 immediately preceding the F7, so it must belong in position 1. C follows B in the alphabet, and position 2 calls for a minor chord, so place Cm7 in position 2. As a result, you can conclude that this progression is in the key of B♭, and you would use the B♭ major scale to solo over it. Use the audio jam track to practice your improvisation using the B♭ major scale.

As further practice, let's fill in the remaining blanks in Fig. 16. D is the third degree of the B♭ major scale, and position 3 requires a minor chord, so Dm7 goes there. Position 4 is major, and E♭ is the fourth scale degree, so place an E♭maj7 chord there. Position 6 is minor, and G follows F, so Gm7 gets the sixth spot. Finally, A is the seventh degree of the B♭ major scale, and position 7 is the half-diminished chord, so Am7♭5 fills that spot.

Got that down? Good. Here are several more progressions containing seventh chords (Figs. 17–19). Fill in the puzzle diagrams for each of these progressions, and then check your answers in the appendix. Remember, a dominant seventh chord can only fit into position 5, and a half-diminished chord only fits into position 7. When you're finished with the analysis, practice jamming over the chord progressions using the major scale associated with each.

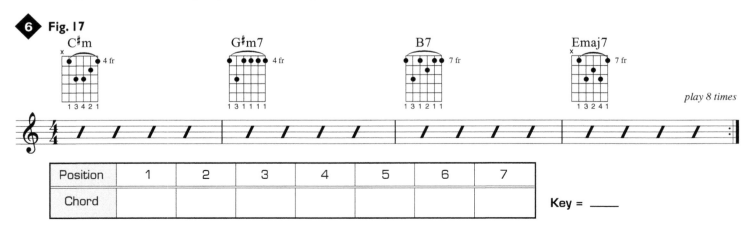

Fig. 17

play 8 times

Position	1	2	3	4	5	6	7
Chord							

Key = _____

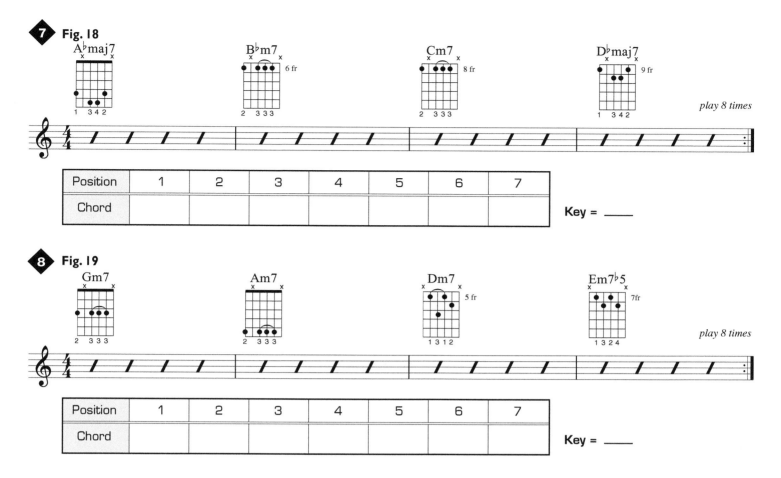

7 Fig. 18

Abmaj7   Bbm7 (6 fr)   Cm7 (8 fr)   Dbmaj7 (9 fr)

play 8 times

Position	1	2	3	4	5	6	7
Chord							

Key = ____

8 Fig. 19

Gm7   Am7   Dm7 (5 fr)   Em7b5 (7fr)

play 8 times

Position	1	2	3	4	5	6	7
Chord							

Key = ____

Extended Chords

Jazz isn't limited only to seventh chords—extended chords play a huge role as well. An extended chord is one that contains notes beyond the seventh degree. The possible extensions are ninths, elevenths, and thirteenths. Check out the C major scale spelled out in Fig. 20 with these scale degrees labeled.

Fig. 20

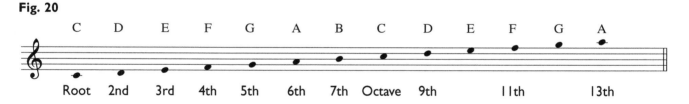

C   D   E   F   G   A   B   C   D   E   F   G   A

Root 2nd 3rd 4th 5th 6th 7th Octave 9th 11th 13th

Notice that the note names of the ninth, eleventh, and thirteenth match the second, fourth, and sixth scale degrees; they're just one octave higher in pitch. Though in strict harmonic theory, these extensions must be played in the higher octave, the reality of the guitar's fretboard layout often dictates that these extensions be played in the same octave.

So, why not simply call a thirteenth chord a sixth chord then? That answer is actually quite simple: For any of these extensions to exist, the seventh scale degree must be present. If there's no seventh, the chord name will reflect that (e.g., C6 instead of C13).

Extended chords can be major, minor, or dominant in quality, but there are rules governing which extensions can have which qualities. For example, you will not likely come across a major eleventh chord. Using the key of C for an example, a Cmaj11 chord would be spelled: C–E–G–B–D–F. In this case, the major third (E) and the eleventh (F) clash to produce a rather unpleasant sound. For this same reason, major or dominant thirteenth chords do not contain the eleventh scale degree.

11

In terms of placing extended chords in their appropriate positions of the puzzle, the extensions don't have much to do with their position; it's the chord *quality* that determines its spot. For example, D9, D11, and D13 are all dominant chords, and where do we put dominant chords in the puzzle? That's right, position 5. Likewise, Dm9 and Dm11 are minor chords, so we know that they would have to fit into position 2, 3, or 6. See how easy this is? Good, let's get some practice analyzing chord progressions that contain extended chords.

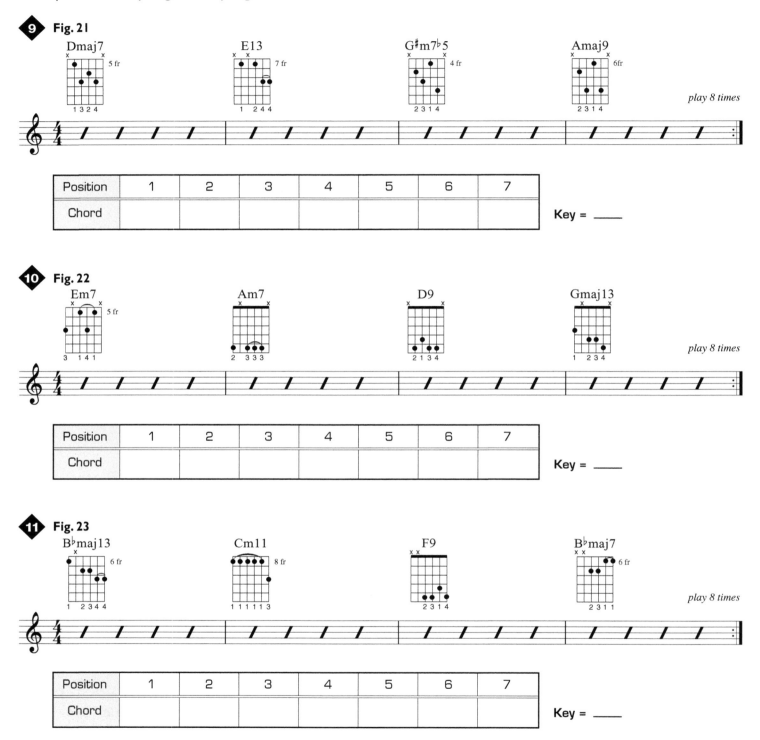

9 **Fig. 21**

Position	1	2	3	4	5	6	7
Chord							

Key = ____

10 **Fig. 22**

Position	1	2	3	4	5	6	7
Chord							

Key = ____

11 **Fig. 23**

Position	1	2	3	4	5	6	7
Chord							

Key = ____

4 Modal Harmony

Thus far, we've used the puzzle system to analyze chord progressions and locate the "one" chord (I), or the major key. Many musicians prefer this method because it's easy to use and requires the knowledge of only one scale: the major scale. Some people, however, prefer to communicate using the names of the major modes. This approach yields the same results; it just utilizes a different terminology. To be sure you fully understand the modes as best you can, let's take a few moments to pore over the names, spellings, and rules that go with the major modes. (Relax, they're not nearly as difficult as everyone thinks!)

By definition, *modes* are scales built upon each note of a central scale. So, just as there are seven notes in a major scale, there are seven modes derived from the major scale. The names of these seven modes are: Ionian, Dorian, Phrygian, Lydian, Mixolydian, Aeolian, and Locrian. It's important to point out that each of these modes is a permutated major scale. That is, the seven modes of C major all contain the same notes; they just start and end on a different pitch (Fig. 24).

```
W = whole step
H = half step
```

C Ionian (same as C major) =
    W W H W W W H
    C D E F G A B C

D Dorian =
    W H W W W H W
    D E F G A B C D

E Phrygian =
    H W W W H W W
    E F G A B C D E

F Lydian =
    W W W H W W H
    F G A B C D E F

G Mixolydian =
    W W H W W H W
    G A B C D E F G

A Aeolian =
    W H W W H W W
    A B C D E F G A

B Locrian =
    H W W H W W W
    B C D E F G A B

Fig. 24 The Modes of C Major

If you examine Fig. 24 closely, you should notice that the whole step/half step intervals change from scale to scale. This provides you with yet another way to understand and analyze the modes. For example, rather than seeing D Dorian and thinking of it as the second mode of C major, you could analyze D Dorian as a D major scale with flatted third and seventh degrees (1–2–♭3–4–5–6–♭7; D–E–F–G–A–B–C). Fig. 25 contains the alterations necessary to create each of the seven modes using this method.

Fig. 25

Ionian:	1–2–3–4–5–6–7
Dorian:	1–2–♭3–4–5–6–♭7
Phrygian:	1–♭2–♭3–4–5–♭6–♭7
Lydian:	1–2–3–♯4–5–6–7
Mixolydian:	1–2–3–4–5–6–♭7
Aeolian:	1–2–♭3–4–5–♭6–♭7
Locrian:	1–♭2–♭3–4–♭5–♭6–♭7

Practice spelling the following scales using this method. The root note is already on the notation staff, and the answers are at the end of the figure. Don't cheat!

Fig. 26

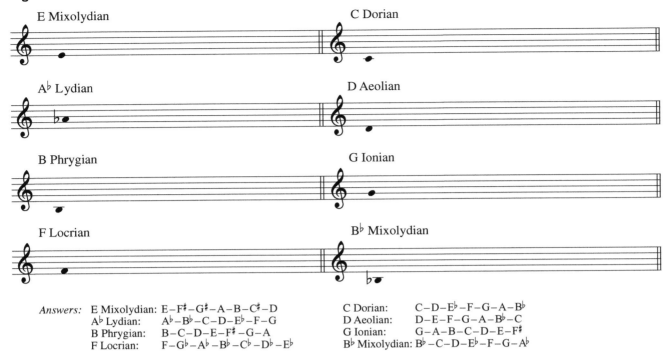

Answers: E Mixolydian: E–F♯–G♯–A–B–C♯–D   C Dorian: C–D–E♭–F–G–A–B♭
            A♭ Lydian: A♭–B♭–C–D–E♭–F–G   D Aeolian: D–E–F–G–A–B♭–C
            B Phrygian: B–C–D–E–F♯–G–A   G Ionian: G–A–B–C–D–E–F♯
            F Locrian: F–G♭–A♭–B♭–C♭–D♭–E♭   B♭ Mixolydian: B♭–C–D–E♭–F–G–A♭

Okay, so how is all this going to help you find the right scale to play over a chord progression? For starters, each mode corresponds directly to its respective note in the major scale. In other words, modes I (Ionian) and IV (Lydian) are major and used over major chords; modes ii (Dorian), iii (Phrygian), and vi (Aeolian) are minor and thus used over minor chords; mode V (Mixolydian) is dominant, so it's used over dominant chords; finally, mode vii (Locrian) can be used over m7♭5 or diminished chords.

Now, let's apply this to a chord progression: F♯m–E–B. Using our previous method, you should be able to determine that this example is a ii–I–V progression in the key of E:

Position	I	2	3	4	5	6	7
Chord	E	F♯m			B		

Fig. 27

Now let's analyze the same progression from a modal perspective. Here, since F♯m is the first chord in the progression and functioning as the "two" chord, we would say that the progression uses the second mode of E major, which is F♯ Dorian. Or, if you want to state the modal names chord-by-chord, we would say that F♯ Dorian is played over the F♯m chord, E Ionian is played over E major, and B Mixolydian is played over B major. What it basically boils down to is that you've got three options when it comes time to play your solo: 1) You could stick with the major scale, E, and use that over the entire progression. 2) You could choose to think of F♯ Dorian as the key and use that as your "one scale fits all." Or, 3) you could follow each chord change individually, shifting modes from F♯ Dorian to E Ionian to B Mixolydian. Listen to Fig. 28 on the audio to hear each of these options demonstrated simply using the appropriate scale. (An E major scale is played the first time through the progression; F♯ Dorian is played the second time; each chord change is followed individually the third time.) After you've listened to those examples, try jamming along with the progression in Fig. 29, experimenting with all three improvisational methods. If you're unfamiliar with the fingerings for the seven modes, Fig. 30 contains one movable pattern for each mode.

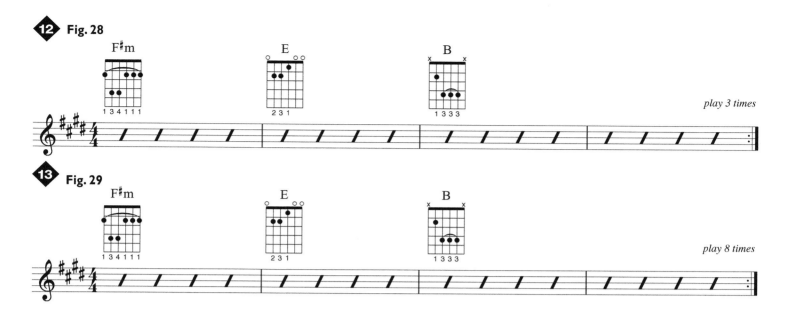

Fig. 28

Fig. 29

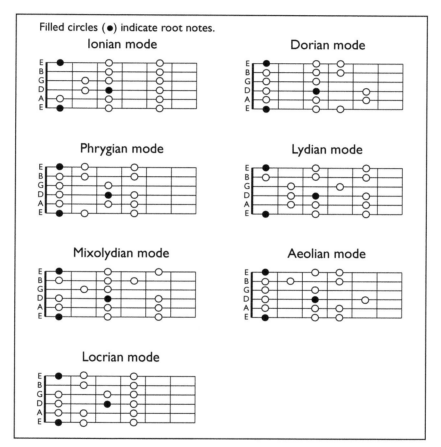

Filled circles (●) indicate root notes.

Ionian mode

Dorian mode

Phrygian mode

Lydian mode

Mixolydian mode

Aeolian mode

Locrian mode

Fig. 30

In case you're still a bit confused, here's a simple three-step guide to determining which mode can be used over any given chord progression.

• **Step 1:** Use the puzzle system to determine the proper numeric placement of each chord.

• **Step 2:** Match the numeric function of the first chord in the progression to its corresponding mode.

• **Step 3:** Name the mode.

Now it's time to test your newfound knowledge of the modes by playing over Figs. 31–34. Use the three-step method above to determine the proper mode to use over each chord progression. Once you've made that assessment, practice jamming over each progression using the jam tracks. While you're jamming, experiment using the three options that were mentioned in Fig. 24. Developing the ability to switch from mode to mode as the music's going will help you later when we discuss chord progressions that contain two or more keys!

14 **Fig. 31**

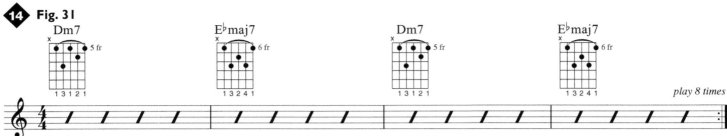

Step 1: iii
Step 2: Dm7 is the first chord and is functioning as the iii chord. Phrygian is the third mode.
Step 3: D Phrygian

15 **Fig. 32**

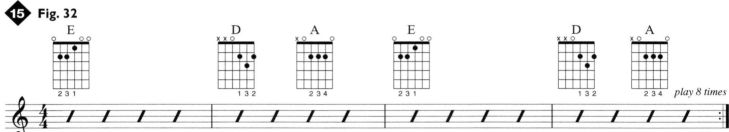

Step 1: V
Step 2: E is the first chord and is functioning as the V chord. Mixolydian is the fifth mode.
Step 3: E Mixolydian

16 **Fig. 33**

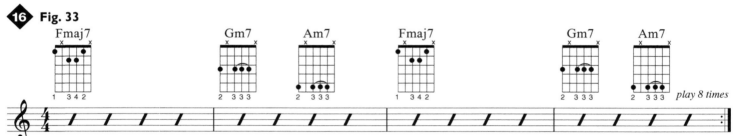

Step 1: I
Step 2: Fmaj7 is the first chord and is functioning as the I chord. Ionian is the first mode.
Step 3: F Ionian

17 **Fig. 34**

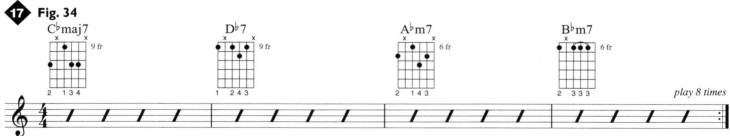

Step 1: IV
Step 2: C♭maj7 is the first chord and is functioning as the IV chord. Lydian is the fourth mode.
Step 3: C♭ Lydian

5 Minor Scale Harmony

Natural Minor

So far, all the methods for determining scale-chord relationships that we've discussed have been based on the major scale. Even modal harmony is based on the major scale. However, I'm sure that at some point in your musical career, you've heard something like, "This tune's in the key of A minor." So, how does the puzzle system work for minor keys?

In the majority of popular music, when we say that a song or chord progression is in a minor key, we are actually referring to the sixth major mode, Aeolian, which is also called the "natural" minor scale. Rather than getting confused at this point, let it be a comforting fact because it means that we are once again working off one of the major modes; we're just going to realign the puzzle system a bit. (*Note: In jazz music, minor keys are harmonized using the harmonic minor scale. We'll discuss this in detail in the chapter on harmonic minor.)

Let's dive right in by first harmonizing an A natural minor scale in both triads and in seventh chords (Fig. 35).

Fig. 35

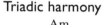

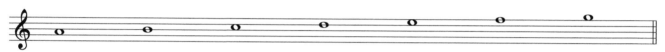

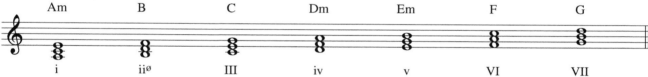

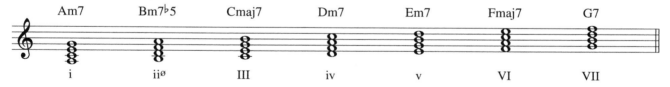

Now, take a look at the two puzzle systems in Fig. 36 to see how the chord qualities have shifted with regard to position.

Fig. 36A

Triadic harmony: major

Position	I	ii	iii	IV	V	vi	vii
Chord	C	Dm	Em	F	G	A	B

Triadic harmony: minor

Position	i	ii	III	iv	v	VI	VII
Chord	Am	B	C	Dm	Em	F	G

Fig. 36B

Seventh chord harmony: major

Position	I	ii	iii	IV	V7	vi	viiø
Chord	Cmaj7	Dm7	Em7	Fmaj7	G7	Am7	Bm7♭5

Seventh chord harmony: minor

Position	i	iiø	III	iv	v	VI	VII
Chord	Am7	Bm7♭5	Cmaj7	Dm7	Em7	Fmaj7	G7

Notice that the major chords have shifted from positions 1, 4, and 5 to 3, 6, and 7, respectively. The minor chords shifted from positions 2, 3, and 6 to 1, 4, and 5, respectively. The diminished chord moved from position 7 to position 2. Although the chord qualities shifted position, their interrelationships haven't really changed at all. As we said before, the natural minor scale is the same as the sixth major mode. Why is that special? Well, as you assign chords to their proper position within the puzzle system, you can use some of the same rules as with major keys. For example, in the major system, we know that there's a half step between the third and fourth positions and between the seventh and root positions. In the minor system, you just slide the half-step intervals over two spots so that they occur between the fifth and sixth positions and between the second and third positions. In the major system, the only place two major chords could appear successively was in positions 4 and 5. Now, if you see two major chords in alphabetical succession in a minor key, you know that they belong in positions 6 and 7.

The end result of these relationships is that the Aeolian mode (natural minor) and the Ionian mode (major) are considered *relative* to each other. So A minor, for example, is the relative minor of C major, and if you start on the third degree of the A minor scale, you'll spell a C major scale. This means that when you're confronted with a natural minor key, you can either play the minor scale of the tonic, or you can simply move up one and a half steps from the tonic and use the resultant major scale in your improvisation.

Let's work through the example in Fig. 37 to determine both the minor and its relative major key. Remember, the same basic principles of the puzzle system apply for minor keys as major keys; for instance, the chords must be organized both alphabetically and according to quality.

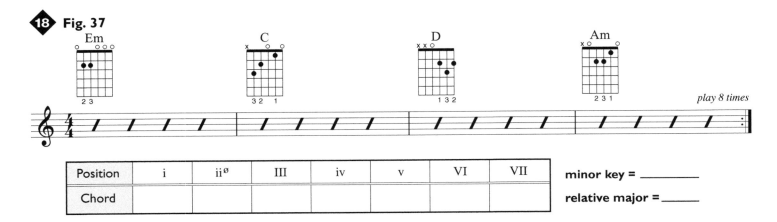

18 **Fig. 37**

Position	i	ii⌀	III	iv	v	VI	VII
Chord							

minor key = _____

relative major = _____

In this example, we see two major chords, C and D, that follow alphabetically. Looking at the minor key puzzle system, positions 6 and 7 require major chords, so we'll place C in position 6 and D in position 7. Since E follows D in the alphabet, and position 1 is a minor chord, we can place the Em chord there. We now know that the progression is in the key of E minor, but let's place the Am chord for practice. If you walk up the puzzle alphabetically, you'll find that Am belongs in position 4. Now, let's fill in the blanks. F# follows E, so position 2 contains an F#° chord. G follows F#, so a G major chord belongs in position 3. Finally, position 5 is a minor chord, and B follows A, so Bm goes there.

So, what is the relative major key of E minor? Simply move up one and a half steps from the note E, or move two positions to the right in the puzzle, and you can conclude that G major is the relative major key. This means you can play either an E minor scale or a G major scale over this particular chord progression.

Try your hand at analyzing the following minor chord progressions using triads (Figs. 38–39) and seventh chords (Figs. 40–41). Place the chords in their proper puzzle positions, identify the tonic minor scale, and also determine its relative major scale as well.

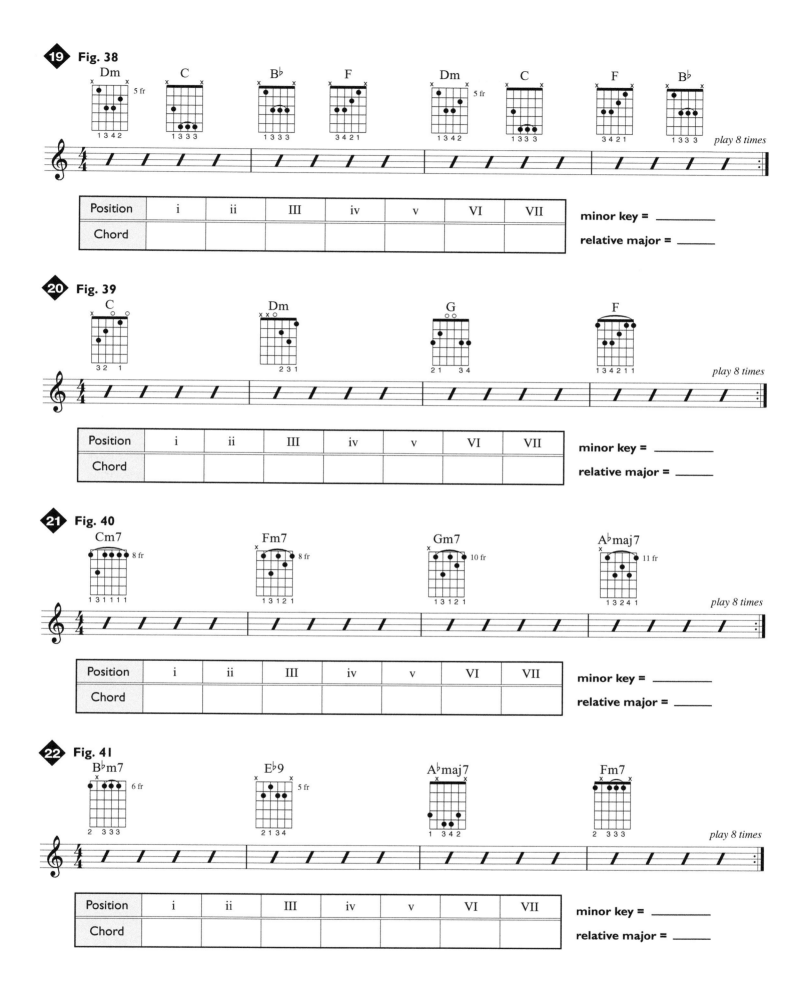

19 **Fig. 38**

Position	i	ii	III	iv	v	VI	VII
Chord							

minor key = _____

relative major = _____

20 **Fig. 39**

Position	i	ii	III	iv	v	VI	VII
Chord							

minor key = _____

relative major = _____

21 **Fig. 40**

Position	i	ii	III	iv	v	VI	VII
Chord							

minor key = _____

relative major = _____

22 **Fig. 41**

Position	i	ii	III	iv	v	VI	VII
Chord							

minor key = _____

relative major = _____

6 Power Chords

Thus far, we've analyzed the scale-chord relationships in terms of triadic and seventh chord harmony. There's another very common chord type that needs our attention as well: the *power chord*. A power chord, also called a "5" chord, consists of the root and the fifth degree of the major scale. Because there's no third, a power chord by itself is neither major nor minor. In the context of a chord progression, however, major or minor tonality can be implied. Let's revisit the C major scale, and we'll harmonize it using power chords.

Fig. 42

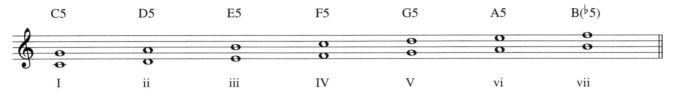

You'll notice that underneath the scale, I've filled in chord qualities according to the major scale puzzle system, which is exactly the method you'll use to determine the key of a power-chord progression.

You should also have noticed that the seventh degree contains a flatted 5th. Though this is harmonically correct, you will more typically see a perfect 5th used in practice. No need to worry, however, as that chord is rarely used in strict harmonic context in rock or pop music anyway. More on that in later chapters.

Let's work through a typical power-chord progression to determine both its overall tonality and the scale you should use for your solo.

Fig. 43

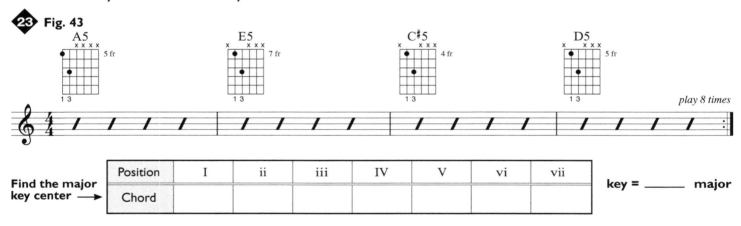

Find the major key center →

Position	I	ii	iii	IV	V	vi	vii
Chord							

key = _____ major

In the above progression, you could theoretically place the chords in any puzzle position as long as you maintain alphabetical order. However, most of these random organizations will sound horrible once you start to improvise using the key center dictated by the puzzle. In a progression such as this, there are really only two possible correct tonal centers: one minor, one major. And these will actually contain the same notes, just starting at a different point in the scale. The trick is to look for musical commonalities in addition to the other puzzle rules you've learned. For example, the I–IV–V is perhaps the most common chord progression in popular music, and it just so happens that three of the four chords in Fig. 34 fit into those positions while maintaining the alphabetical requirement. D5 and E5 follow each other alphabetically and are one whole step apart, so let's try those in positions 4 and 5. Working backward, C♯5 is a half step below D5, so it fits in position 3. Moving down another two whole steps, we determine that A5 fits into position 1, and the tonal center is A major. Now, try jamming over the progression using the A major scale.

The progression below has a minor key tonal center. See if you can figure this one out on your own.

24 **Fig. 44**

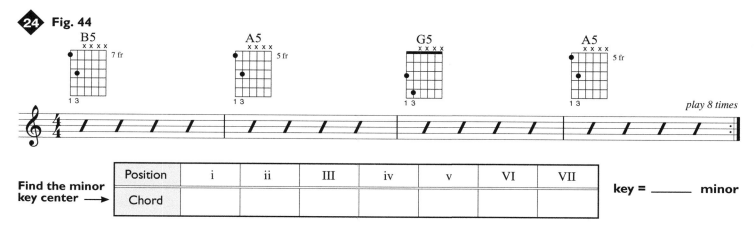

Position	i	ii	III	iv	v	VI	VII
Find the minor key center → Chord							

key = _____ minor

Sometimes, it's impossible to determine whether a progression has a major or minor tonality (unless a bassist or keyboardist is providing some type of tonal definition). In these cases, it's entirely up to you to interpret it any way you'd like. Take, for example, the E5–A5 progression in Fig. 45. This progression can be treated as either major or minor. Additionally, you have the choice between treating either E or A as the root! So, there are *four* choices available: A major, A minor, E major, and E minor.

To really have some fun, try playing the first four choruses using an E major scale, the next two choruses with an E minor scale, and the final two choruses again with the an E major scale. This switching between parallel major and minor keys is termed *modulation* and is quite an effective improvisation tool when faced with a very simple harmony such as this.

25 **Fig. 45**

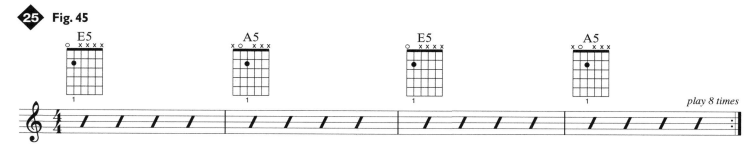

Finally, you might encounter power chords mixed in with regular triads or seventh chords. In this case, simply proceed using the normal puzzle system and place the power chords in the proper position, allowing the position to dictate the implied tonality (major or minor) of the power chord. Analyze the following progression in for practice.

26 **Fig. 46**

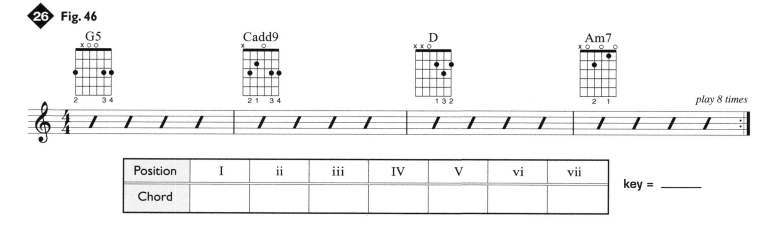

Position	I	ii	iii	IV	V	vi	vii
Chord							

key = _____

7 Blues Progressions

It's time to start breaking a few of the rules you've learned so far. One of the most popular music forms over which to solo is the 12-bar blues. Typically consisting of a I–IV–V chord progression, the 12-bar form is generally arranged in the following manner: four bars of I, two bars of IV, two bars of I, one bar of V, one bar of IV, one and a half bars of I, and a turnaround made up of a half bar of V. The difference, however, between a blues I–IV–V and a normal I–IV–V is that in the blues, each chord has a dominant quality. For example, a I–IV–V progression in the key of E would be E–A–B. In the blues, however, we make each chord dominant, resulting in an E7–A7–B7 set of changes.

27 **Fig. 47**

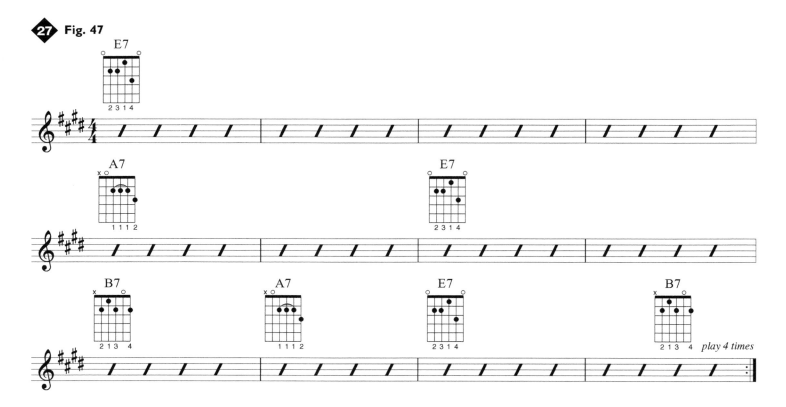

When it comes time to solo, this all-dominant progression presents a new challenge. We can't simply use the major scale of the I chord (E7) over the entire progression. If you'll think back to our chapter on the major modes, you should remember that the Mixolydian mode is used over a dominant seventh chord. So, how about using the E Mixolydian mode over the progression? Well, that has problems as well. For example, G♯ is the third degree of the E Mixolydian mode, and if you were to play that note over the A7 chord, it would wreak aural havoc with the G natural that is the seventh degree of the A7 chord.

Okay, how about switching back and forth between the E, A, and B Mixolydian modes over the E7, A7, and B7 chords, respectively. That will work just fine, but it's also a lot of work. Instead, you might want to try a new type of scale: either the minor pentatonic or the blues scale.

Fig. 48

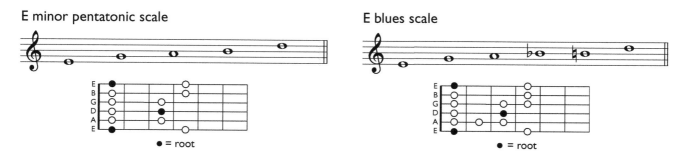

E minor pentatonic scale

E blues scale

• = root

The minor pentatonic takes its name from the fact that it has a flatted third degree and contains only five notes (1–♭3–4–5–♭7). The blues scale is identical to the minor pentatonic but also includes the flatted fifth degree—sometimes referred to as a "blue note." When using the blues scale, be sure not to linger on or resolve to the flatted fifth, as its main function is to serve as a tension-producing passing tone.

The two fingering patterns provided in Fig. 48 are the most common for both scales. In the key of E, you would play these either in open position or at the 12th fret. Use audio track 27 as accompaniment to practice using these scales for your blues solos. Be sure to practice playing in both positions, as open position definitely has a different "feel."

Try your hand at the following two 12-bar blues arrangements. First identify the I7–IV7–V7 chords, then use either the minor pentatonic or the blues scale that corresponds with the I chord.

Fig. 49

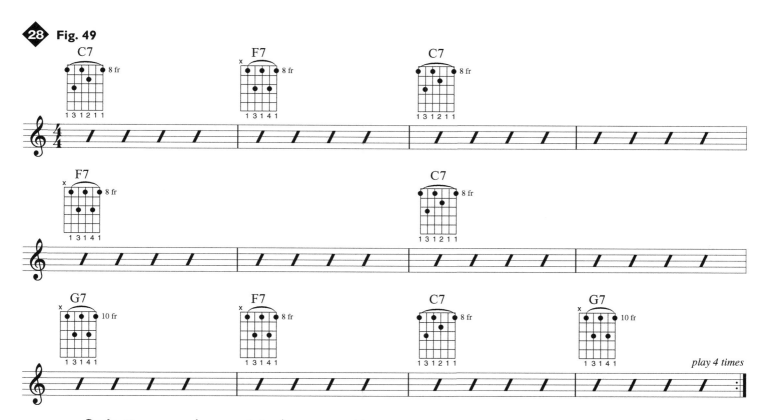

Scale = _____ minor pentatonic or _____ blues.

Fig. 50

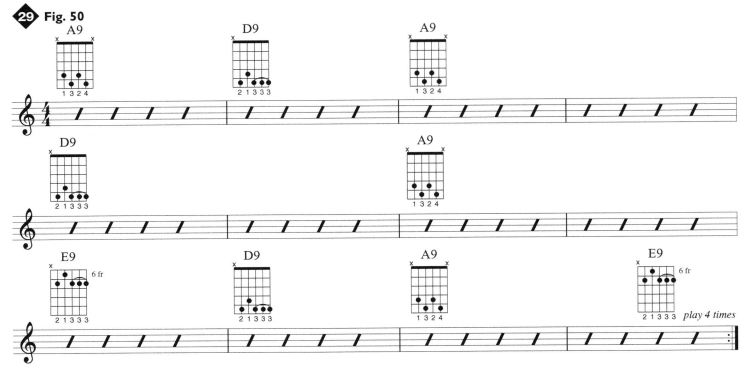

Scale = _____ minor pentatonic or _____ blues.

As you may have guessed, it's possible to have a *minor* blues progression, too. In a minor blues, the chord progression is still a I–IV–V, but we add the "m7" symbol to the I and IV chords: Im7–IVm7–V7. As in a standard blues, you should use either a minor pentatonic scale or the blues scale over the minor blues progression. Again, first identify the Im7–IVm7–V7 chords, and use the scale that corresponds to the Im7 chord. Try jamming over the following minor blues.

30 **Fig. 51**

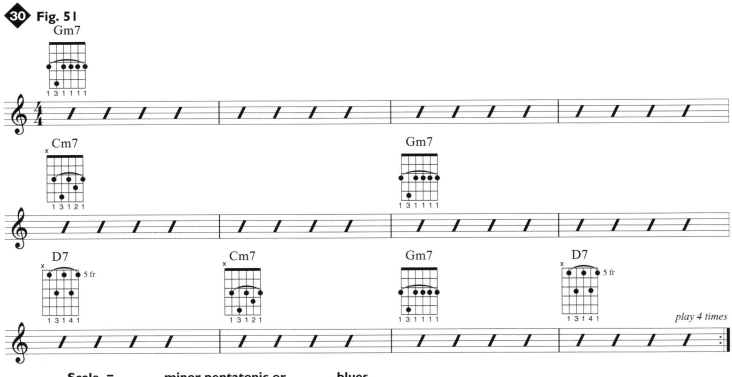

Scale = _____ minor pentatonic or _____ blues.

Finally, you may encounter a blues form that mixes minor, major, and dominant chords. A classic example of this is B.B. King's "The Thrill Is Gone." This next example is similar to B.B.'s blues classic. Listen to the jam track and try to identify the tonal center. You may find the puzzle system helpful for determining which minor pentatonic or blues scale to use with this progression. *Hint: This is a minor blues, so be sure to use the puzzle system that accomodates a Im chord.

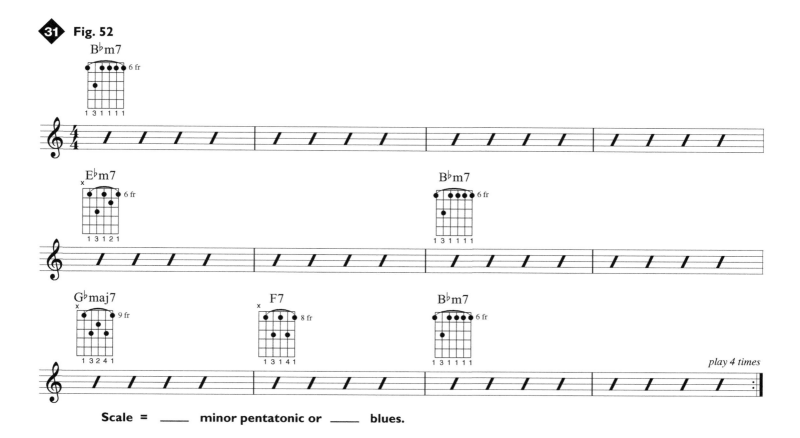

Scale = _____ minor pentatonic or _____ blues.

8 Riffs & Arpeggios

A fair amount of recorded music, especially in rock and pop, contains riffs and arpeggios in the harmony as opposed to plucked or strummed chords. If you're given the chord symbols above the staff, you can plug those into the puzzle system and find your scale. If not, you'll need to do a little more grunt work, but it's really quite easy. Simply collect the notes from the arpeggiated figure or the riff and arrange them into one common key or scale. Let's take a look at the arpeggiated figure below.

 Fig. 53

Start by writing down each new note in the progression. The first note is A. The second note is A, so skip to the next one, which is C. The next new note is G. Then there's a D, an F#, and finally, a B. Now, let's put those in alphabetical order, starting with the A: A–B–C–D–F#–G. These notes give us an A Dorian, or G major, scale (minus the E). As a result, it's safe to say that you could use the A Dorian mode or the G major scale over this progression. Try one of these scales with the accompanying jam track. Then move on to the following examples for more practice in determining the scale to use over riff-based harmony.

 Fig. 54

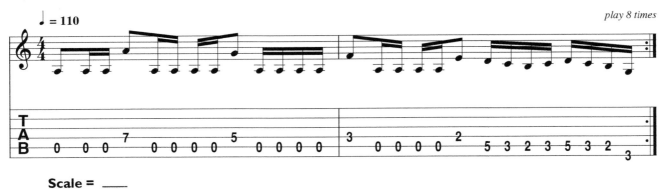

Scale = ____

 Fig. 55

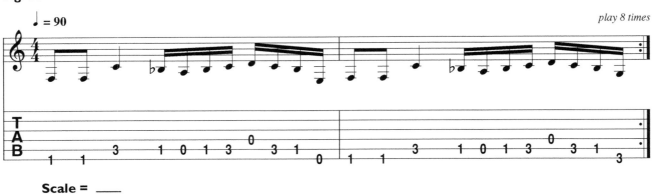

Scale = ____

9 Nondiatonic Harmony

Until now, most of the examples in this book have had "one-scale-fits-all" solutions. The reality in music is that there are often nondiatonic chords—and even key changes—within songs. If, for example, a nondiatonic chord is present for only a brief portion of the song and acting as a passing chord, you can simply choose to ignore it. However, anything more than that, and you're going to need a strategy.

Though it's not really nondiatonic harmony, modulation is a popular tool used to add an uplifting feel to a section. One of the simplest modulations, from an improvisational viewpoint, is when the modulation takes place between solo sections. Say, for example, you have a 32-bar solo, and the first sixteen measures are in the key of C, and the last sixteen measures are in the key of D. Check out the example below.

35 Fig. 56

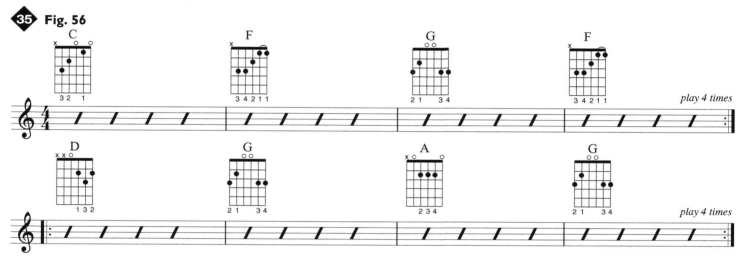

In this situation, you would simply divide the section into diatonic groupings, that is, successive chords that belong to the same key. Here, it was easy because the key change divided the section into two parts; so you'd play a C major scale over the first sixteen measures and a D major scale over the final sixteen measures.

Sometimes, however, it's not so cut and dried. For example, it's common in jazz songs to employ chords that are not diatonic to the key. Though you could change scales with each and every chord change, they often move by quite quickly, making that kind of improvisational juggling act very difficult. On the other hand, if you can group two or three or more chords together into one key, switching scales every few measures is much more appealing than with every chord change. Let's take a look at the progression below.

36 Fig. 57

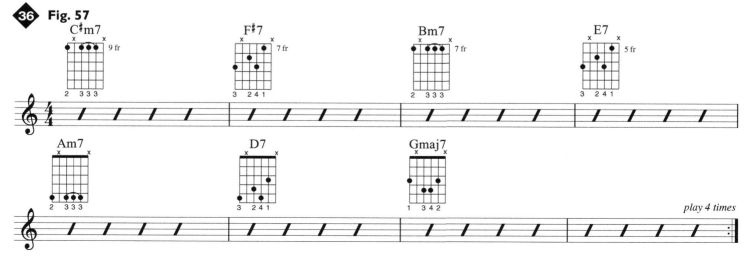

Now, before we analyze the preceding chord progression, I'm going to give you a huge tip that will help you tremendously when improvising over jazz progressions. Notice that there are three sets of chords where a dominant seventh follows a minor seventh. Further, the intervallic distance between each minor and dominant seventh is a perfect fourth. Almost 98.9% of the time you see a dominant seventh follow a minor seventh with a perfect fourth interval between them, you're likely looking at a ii–V progresssion. This is by far the most common chord progression in jazz music. And to determine the key, all you need do is move one whole step back from the ii chord root (e.g., Dm7–G7; key = C major) and play the corresponding major scale. Or, you can simply play the Dorian mode of the ii chord (e.g., Dm7–G7; play D Dorian). Additionally, each new ii–V you come upon signals a change in key, and these become quite easy to recognize with time and practice.

So, looking at Fig. 57, we see three consecutive ii–V progressions, meaning we need to change scales every two measures. Over the C#m7–F#7 changes, you would play C# Dorian or B major; over the Bm7–E7 changes, you'd play B Dorian or A major; over Am7–D7 changes, you'd play A Dorian or G major. Notice that the last ii–V is in the key of G major, and the progression ends with two measures of Gmaj7. This means you can use the G major scale to solo over the final four measures of the progression. For variety, try playing from the G Lydian mode for the final measure leading back to C#m7. Remember, the Lydian mode contains a raised fourth degree, which, in the key of G, is C#, so it helps draw the harmony toward C#m7.

10 Harmonic Minor

The harmonic minor scale was developed by composers who found a basic flaw in the diatonic melodies and harmonies of the natural minor scale. If you'll recall, the natural minor scale contains a flatted seventh degree. This creates a whole step between it and the root, which is not nearly ideal as the half step interval for generating a sense of resolution toward the root. With this in mind, traditional composers based their melodies and harmonies on the natural minor scale with a raised seventh degree, thus defining that note as a leading tone. This harmonic method has since become standard practice in minor jazz progressions as well.

The harmonic minor scale is spelled: 1–2–♭3–4–5–♭6–7. Let's harmonize the A harmonic minor scale and see how the diatonic chords differ from those of the natural minor scale (Fig. 35; p.17).

Fig. 58 Harmonized A harmonic minor scale

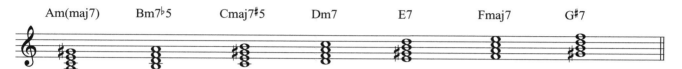

If we examine the two harmonized scales, the two major differences are in positions 5 and 7. In the natural minor scale, position 5 contains a minor seventh chord. The problem with this is that it does not create a strong V–I pull, whereas the dominant seventh chord in the harmonic minor tonality contains a major third (G♯), which is only a half step away from the root of the Im chord (A). This creates a strong resolution to the Im chord. Moving to position 7, the root of the dominant seventh chord (G) in the natural minor harmony is a whole step below the Im chord. By using the harmonic minor scale, the root moves up a half step (G♯) and the quality becomes diminished. This also creates a strong resolution toward the Im chord (Am7).

The other alteration you should have noticed is that the tonic chord (Im) becomes a minor/major seventh chord. While this works as a wonderful embellishment to a regular minor seventh chord in certain situations, it is considered much too dissonant to serve as a tonic chord. So, in practice, the flatted seventh is typically substituted for the natural seventh in the Im chord.

Now, you may be thinking that whenever you see a minor progression in jazz, it's "bombs away" with the harmonic minor scale. Not quite. Since the V7 and VII°7 chords are the only ones affected by the raised seventh degree, you can still use the *natural* minor scale over the other diatonic chords. In the case of the common minor ii–V–i, however, jazzers will tend to blow harmonic minor, or more specifically, Spanish Phrygian, over the entire progression. Spanish Phrygian (Fig. 59) is the fifth mode of harmonic minor, and since all the chord tones in a ii–V–i are found in the harmonic minor scale, you can use it over the whole progression. The only exception is the alteration we made to the i chord. Remember, we flatted the seventh degree, so use the natural seventh in the harmonic minor scale as a passing tone over the i chord, or else it will clash.

Fig. 59 Fingering for Spanish Phrygian scale

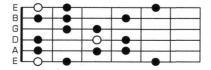

Figs. 60–62 contain several minor jazz progressions. Practice soloing over each of them, using the natural minor and harmonic minor (Spanish Phrygian) scales where appropriate. Notice that the analysis for Fig. 60 has been done for you using both the natural minor and harmonic minor scales. Play it this way the first four times, then try the Spanish Phrygian over the entire progression for the final four choruses. In Figs. 61–62, you'll need to use the puzzle system to determine the minor key. Then, decide when to use the harmonic minor (or Spanish Phrygian) scale in your solo.

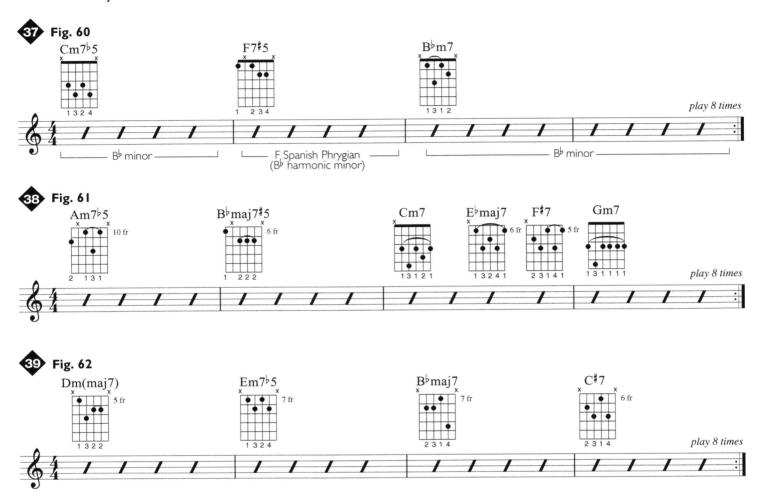

11 Melodic Minor

Jazzers have long been known for their exceptional improvisational talents. This is partially because they are trained to use scales and harmony that fall outside the realm of major modes. You've already discovered the harmonic minor scale in a previous chapter. Now, we're going to learn how and when to use the *melodic minor*, or the "jazz minor" scale.

The harmonic minor scale created a greater pull to resolution by raising the seventh scale degree. However, this move also created a 1½ step interval between the sixth and seventh intervals. The melodic minor scale makes up for this flaw by raising the sixth interval of the natural minor scale as well.

The melodic minor is an interesting scale in that the notes change depending on the direction of the scale. In ascending order, the melodic minor is simply a major scale with flatted third degree (1–2–♭3–4–5–6–7). When descending, the notes match those of the natural minor scale (♭7–♭6–5–4–♭3–2–1).

Fig. 63 A melodic minor scale

The reason for this is that the raised sixth and seventh degrees tend to pull toward resolution at the octave when ascending. In descending order, however, flatting the sixth and seventh degrees creates a downward pull toward the fifth, which is also a strong resolution note. In practice, however, you should employ the melodic minor scale in its ascending form during improvisation.

Now, let's harmonize the A melodic minor scale and examine the chords.

Fig. 64 Harmonized A melodic minor scale

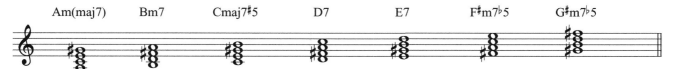

Am(maj7)   Bm7   Cmaj7♯5   D7   E7   F♯m7♭5   G♯m7♭5

As you can see, the melodic minor provides a slightly different set of diatonic seventh chords than either the natural or harmonic minor. One of the most important changes is that the chord in position 4 is now a dominant seventh chord. Thus far, you've learned that when confronted with a dominant seventh chord in the harmony, the scale of choice is the Mixolydian mode, or the major scale of the chord root that is a perfect fifth below the root of the dominant seventh chord (e.g., for D7, play either D Mixolydian or G major). Now, you can also use the melodic minor of the chord root that is a perfect fourth below the root of the dominant seventh chord (e.g., for D7, use A melodic minor). Modally speaking, you'd play the fourth mode of A melodic minor, which is the D Lydian dominant scale. As the name implies, the Lydian dominant contains a raised fourth degree (G♯ in the key of D), which serves as a strong leading tone to the 5th (A) of the D7 chord.

Also, the chord in position 6 has changed from a major seventh to a half-diminished (m7♭5) chord. This means that you now have another option for soloing over a half-diminished chord. Previously, you used either the Locrian mode, or the major scale a half step above the root.

Now, you can use the melodic minor scale of the chord root one and a half steps above the half-diminished chord root (e.g., for F#m7♭5, use A melodic minor).

Try soloing over the progression below. Note that there's a nondiatonic dominant chord in the progression that contains a #11 (or #4, are you thinking Lydian dominant yet?). There is also a ii–V conveniently tossed in over which the rules say you should play D Dorian. However, if you're feeling harmonically adventurous, use Dorian for the first two choruses, but try D melodic minor for the final two. Fig. 65 contains fingering patterns for the melodic minor and Lydian dominant scales in case you're not familiar with them.

Fig. 65A   Melodic Minor Scale (movable pattern)   **Fig. 65B**   Lydian Dominant Scale (movable pattern)

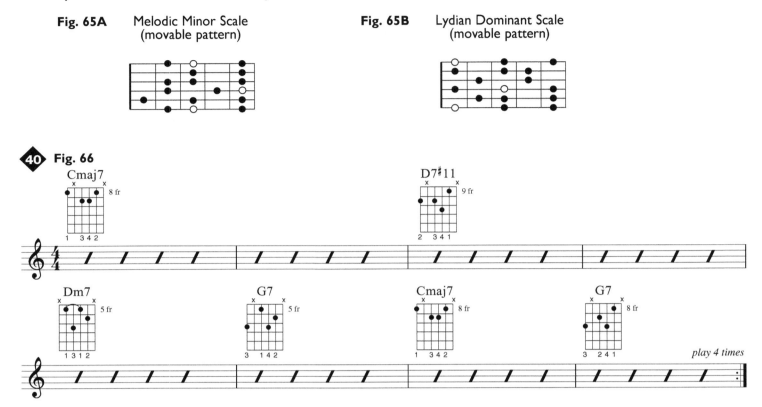

There's yet another common use for the melodic minor scale—over altered dominant chords. As we've already seen, the melodic minor scale is quite popular in the jazz genre, and there is an abundance of altered dominant chords in jazz chord progressions. Altered dominant chords are defined as having either the fifth degree or the ninth degree raised or flatted: ♭5 (#11), #5 (♭13), ♭9, #9. By building a scale from an altered dominant chord, we get the altered scale.

Fig. 67 C Altered Scale

Since the altered scale is the seventh mode of melodic minor, you can use the melodic minor scale that is one half step above the chord root. So, for example, over a C7♭9 or a C7♭13(♭9) chord, you could play D♭ melodic minor (C altered scale). The following chord progression provides a wonderful setting for improv with the melodic minor scale. A quick analysis informs us that the first three measures make up a ii–V–i progression, with the C9♯11 in measure 4 acting as the IV chord in the key of G minor. Using our rule for playing over altered dominant chords, we would play the D altered, or the E♭ melodic minor scale, over the D7♯9 and D7♭9 chords. Then, over the C9♯11, we can revisit our friend, the C Lydian dominant scale.

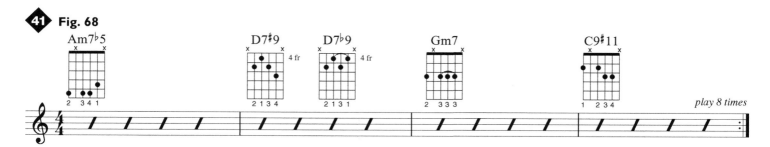

Fig. 68

12 Symmetrical scales

Scales are built on patterns of intervals (e.g., major = WWHWWWH; minor = WHWWHWW). Scales that are built on a repetitive pattern of intervals are called *symmetrical* scales. There are three symmetrical scales that are commonly used in popular music: *chromatic, whole tone,* and *diminished.*

Chromatic Scale

The *chromatic* scale contains all twelve tones of Western music arranged in half-step intervals. In ascending order, the tones are notated with sharps; in descending order, they're notated with flats.

Fig. 69 C chromatic Scale

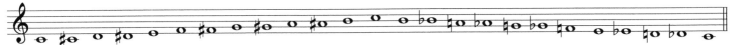

Because the chromatic scale contains all twelve tones, there is no true tonal center—any note can serve as the tonic. Due to its atonal nature, the chromatic scale exists more in theory than in practice. Typically, we borrow nondiatonic tones from the chromatic scale to use in conjunction with tones of a major or minor scale to create color and tension.

Whole Tone Scale

The *whole tone* scale gets its name from its construction—built entirely of whole steps. Because of this, the whole tone scale contains only six notes; this also means that one letter representation will be missing from the scale. It doesn't matter which letter you omit, as long as you maintain whole-step intervals. Also due to this construction, there are only two whole tone scales. That is, the C whole tone scale contains the same notes as the D, E, F#, G#, and B♭ whole tone scales, and the B whole tone scale contains the same notes as the C#, D#, F, G, and A whole tone scales. The starting pitches vary, but scale tones are the same. Below is the C whole tone scale; the letter A is missing in its spelling.

Fig. 70 Whole Tone Scales

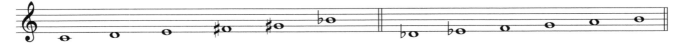

Let's take a closer look at the whole tone scale and proceed to label the chord tones represented in the scale to determine when to use it in your improvisations.

Fig. 71 Whole Tone Scale

Root   9   3   #11/♭5   #5/♭13   ♭7

Notice that the root, third, and flatted seventh are contained in the whole tone scale. This implies a dominant seventh tonality. Additionally, both alterations of the fifth degree are present (♭5 and #5). Enharmonically, these are also sometimes represented as the #11 and ♭13, respectively. Thus, the whole tone scale can be used over any dominant chord with an altered fifth (e.g., C7♭5, C9♭13). Notice that the ninth is unaltered in this scale, so using the whole tone scale over a dominant chord with an altered ninth (e.g., C7♭9) is ill-advised. Practice soloing over the following chord progressions, using the whole tone scale over the appropriate altered dominant chords.

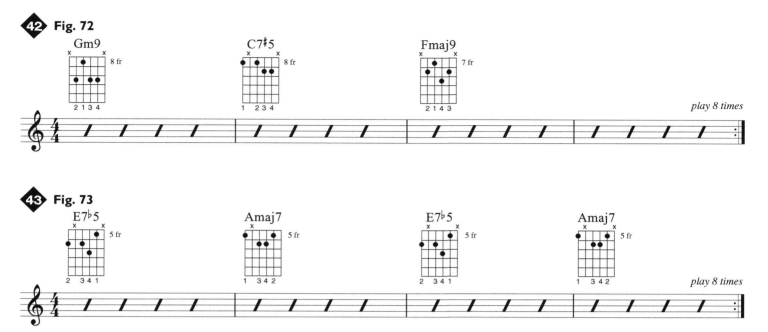

42 **Fig. 72**

43 **Fig. 73**

Dimished Scale

The final symmetrical scale is the *diminished* scale, which is constructed by alternating whole and half steps. This alternating pattern results in two variations: the *whole-half* and the *half-whole*.

Fig. 74A   Whole-Half Diminished Scale   **Fig. 74B**   Half-Whole Diminished Scale

The diminished scale has two main functions. The first is to serve as a scale for use over a diminished chord. If you'll recall the chapters on seventh-chord and modal harmony, position 7 of the puzzle system contains a diminished (or half-diminished) chord. Whether this chord is serving as the vii° or simply as a passing chord, the diminished scale can be used over it. In this case, you'll want to use the whole-half version of the scale, as this version contains all four notes of the diminished seventh chord. Try using the whole-half diminished scale over the diminished chords in the following progression.

44 **Fig. 75**

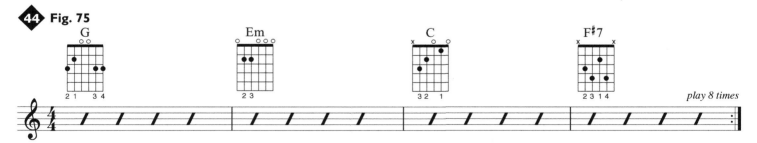

The other scenario for using the diminished scale is to help create an even stronger resolution to the I chord by using it over the V7 chord in a progression. Harmonically, the V7 wants to resolve to the I chord, and though chord substitution theory is the topic for another book, we'll discuss it briefly here.

In diatonic chord theory, the V7 and the vii° chords both belong in the dominant family—meaning they both want to resolve to the I chord. Therefore, the vii° can be substituted for the V7 chord in a progression. This same basic strategy then enables the inventive soloist to use the diminished scale over an altered V7 chord as a means to create a strong drive toward resolution.

Let's rewrite the half-whole diminished scale from Fig. 75, this time labeling the chord tones.

Fig. 76 Half-Whole Diminished Scale

Notice that both altered ninths (♭9, ♯9) and the flatted fifth (♯11) are included in this scale. Therefore, the half-whole diminished scale can be used over a dominant chord with an altered ninth (C7♭9, C7♯9). Though it also appears that you could use the scale over a dominant chord with a flatted fifth (C7♭5), the altered (seventh mode of melodic minor) or whole tone scales are typically used over these chords. Try your hand improvising with the half-whole diminished scale over the appropriate chords in the progressions below. The first is marked for you; you'll have to work through the second on your own.

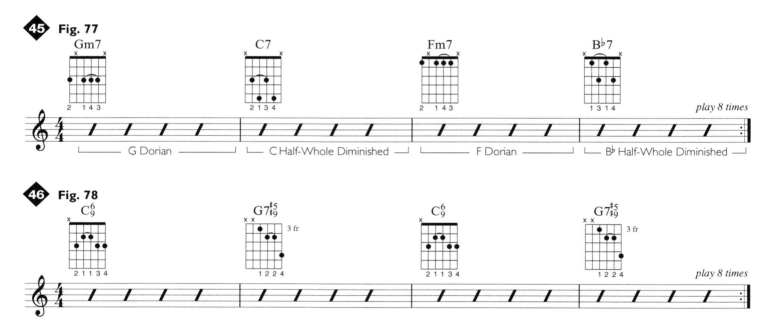

13 Exotic scales

To conclude *Scale Chord Relationships,* let's focus a bit on the use of exotic scales in your improvisation. It's not unheard of for guitar teachers to hand out long lists and spellings of exotic scales with names like the Oriental, Hungarian major, and Gypsy minor scales. While many of these have very interesting intervallic relationships and sound cool, most students don't know exactly where to blend them into a solo. In this section, we'll give some basic guidelines as to where some of these scales fit into chord progressions.

To begin, you should examine the scale's structure. Let's write out the scales mentioned in the above paragraph, labeling the scale degrees and chord tones. A fingering diagram is included for each.

Fig. 79

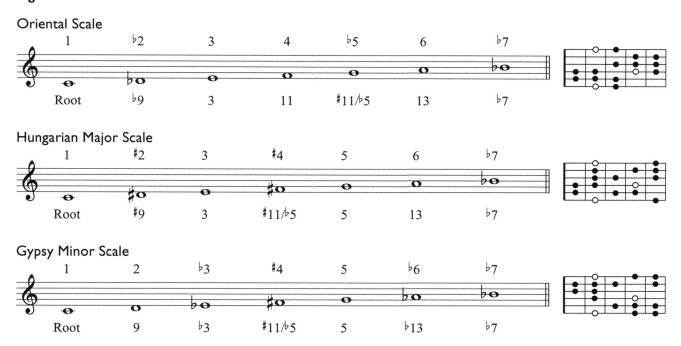

By examining the chord tones inherent in each scale, you can determine over which chords to use these exotic scales (or any others you wish to explore). The first two scale degrees you should look to are the third and the seventh. These two degrees will tell you whether the scale is minor, major, or dominant in quality. From there, examine the other chord tones to search out alterations. For example, if you examine the Gypsy minor scale, you'll see that the third and seventh are both flatted. This indicates that you could use this scale over a minor seventh chord. Further, the ninth is unaltered, and both alterations of the fifth (♭5, ♯5) are present, so this means that you can use this scale over any minor seventh or minor ninth chord with an altered fifth. (Cm7♭5, Cm9♭13). Here, in short, is the method for matching exotic scales to chords:

- Label the chord tones in the scale.
- Find the third and seventh scale degrees.
- Determine the chord quality (maj., min., dom.) from the third and seventh degrees.
- Examine the remaining chord and scale tones.
- Determine the potential chord alterations.
- Jam away!

Like any other scales, exotic scales can be harmonized and they have their own modes. Harmonizing and finding the modes of your favorite exotic scales is not only a wonderful exercise, but will also help you more quickly recognize situations in which you can apply those scales.

Following is a chord progression for each of the three exotic scales we examined in this chapter. The sections are clearly labeled as to when and where to use the exotic scales.

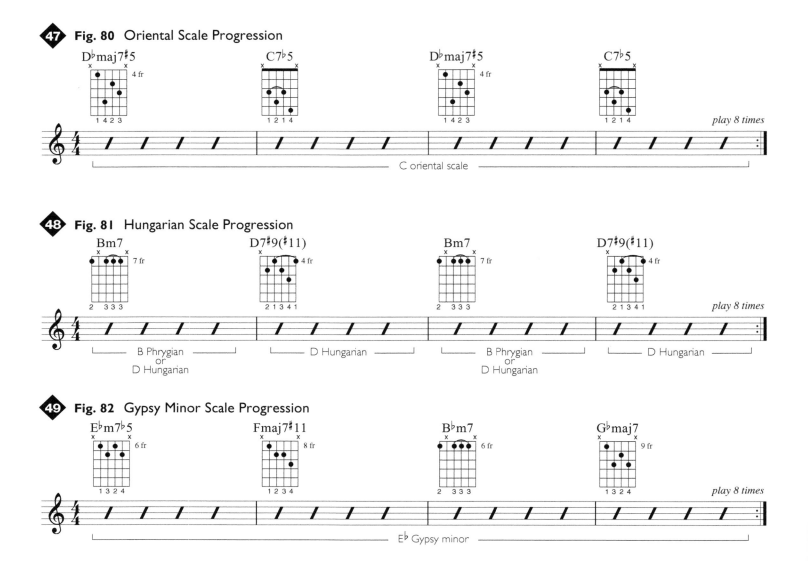

47 **Fig. 80** Oriental Scale Progression

48 **Fig. 81** Hungarian Scale Progression

49 **Fig. 82** Gypsy Minor Scale Progression

Closing

That brings us to the end of *Scale Chord Relationships*. We hope you found the book helpful and insightful. As you come up with other ideas, try recording your own chord progressions, and then play along with your own jam tracks as well as the ones we've provided here. Good luck in your improvisational endeavors, practice hard, and even though we discussed a lot of rules in this book, remember this above all else: if it sounds good, play it.

Appendix

Answers:

Fig. 10

Position	1	2	3	4	5	6	7
Chord	E	F♯m	G♯m	A	B	C♯m	D♯

Key = __E__

Fig. 11

Position	1	2	3	4	5	6	7
Chord	B♭	Cm	Dm	E♭	F	Gm	A

Key = __B♭__

Fig. 12

Position	1	2	3	4	5	6	7
Chord	D	Em	F♯m	G	A	Bm	C♯

Key = __D__

Fig. 17

Position	1	2	3	4	5	6	7
Chord	Emaj7	F♯m7	G♯m7	Amaj7	B7	C♯m7	D♯m7♭5

Key = __E__

Fig. 18

Position	1	2	3	4	5	6	7
Chord	A♭maj7	B♭m7	Cm7	D♭maj7	E♭7	Fm7	Gm7♭5

Key = __A♭__

Fig. 19

Position	1	2	3	4	5	6	7
Chord	Fmaj7	Gm7	Am7	B♭maj7	C7	Dm7	Em7♭5

Key = __F__

Fig. 21

Position	1	2	3	4	5	6	7
Chord	Amaj7	Bm7	C♯m7	Dmaj7	E13	F♯m7	G♯m7♭5

Key = __A__

Fig. 22

Position	1	2	3	4	5	6	7
Chord	Gmaj13	Am7	Bm7	Cmaj7	D9	Em7	F♯m7♭5

Key = __G__

Fig. 23

Position	1	2	3	4	5	6	7
Chord	B♭maj13 / B♭maj7	Cm11	Dm7	E♭maj7	F9	Gm7	Am7♭5

Key = __B♭__

Fig. 38

Position	i	ii	♭III	iv	v	♭VI	♭VII
Chord	Dm	E	F	Gm	Am	B♭	C

minor key = __D__   relative major = __F__

Fig. 39

Position	i	ii	III	iv	v	VI	VII
Chord	Am	B	C	Dm	Em	F	G

minor key = __A__   relative major = __C__

Fig. 40

Position	i	iiø	III	iv	v	VI	VII
Chord	Cm7	Dm7♭5	E♭maj7	Fm7	Gm7	A♭maj7	B♭7

minor key = __C__   relative major = __E♭__

Fig. 41

Position	i	iiø	III	iv	v	VI	VII
Chord	Fm7	Gm7♭5	A♭maj7	B♭m7	Cm7	D♭maj7	E♭9

minor key = __F__   relative major = __A♭__

Fig. 44

Position	i	ii	III	iv	v	VI	VII
Chord	B5	C♯(♭5)	D5	E5	F♯5	G5	A5

minor key = __B__   relative major = __D__

Fig. 46

Position	i	ii	III	iv	v	VI	VII
Chord	G5	Am7	Bm	Cadd9	D	Em	F

Key = __G__

Answer to Fig. 49: C minor pentatonic or C blues

Answer to Fig. 50: A minor pentatonic or A blues

Answer to Fig. 51: G minor pentatonic or G blues

Answer to Fig. 52: B♭ minor pentatonic or B♭ blues

Answer to Fig. 54: Notes = A, B, C, D, E, F, G;   Scale = A minor

Answer to Fig. 55: Notes = F, G, A, B♭, C, D, E;   Scale = F major

Answer to Fig. 61: | Gm7♭5 | B♭maj7♯5 | Cm7 | E♭maj7 F♯7 | Gm7 |
  └─── G minor ───┘ └─ G Harmonic minor ─┘ └ G minor ┘ └─ G Harmonic minor ─┘ └─── G minor ───┘

Answer to Fig. 62: | Dm(maj7) | Em7♭5 | B♭maj7 | C♯7 |
  └─ D Harmonic minor ─┘ └────── D minor ──────┘ └─ D harmonic minor ─┘

Answer to Fig. 78: | C⁶/₉ | G7♯5/♯9 | Cm7 E♭maj7 F♯7 | Gm7 |
  └─── C major ───┘ └─ G half-whole dim. ─┘ └─── C major ───┘ └─ G half-whole dim. ─┘